Super Safari 2

Pupil's Book

Herbert Puchta   Günter Gerngross   Peter Lewis-Jones

CAMBRIDGE
UNIVERSITY PRESS

Map of the book

Hello! (pages 4–7)

Vocabulary	Chant: Grammar
Mike, Gina, Polly, Leo	What's your name? I'm …
▶ **Total physical response:** Say 'hello', Smile, Shake hands, High five	▶ **Song: Hello!**

1 My school (pages 8–15)

Vocabulary	Chant: Grammar	Story and value	CLIL	Thinking skills
board, paper, computer, desk, crayon, pencil case	This is my (crayon).	*The medals* Appreciating differences	Move your body	Sorting
▶ **Total physical response:** Open your book, Pick up your crayon, Draw a picture, Oh no! It's broken			▶ **Song: I've got a pencil case on my desk.**	

2 My body (pages 16–23)

Vocabulary	Chant: Grammar	Story and value	CLIL	Thinking skills
arms, hands, feet, legs, body, head	I can (clap my hands).	*Ouch!* Looking after someone	Animal bodies	Noticing details
▶ **Total physical response:** Kick a ball, It's a goal, Clap your hands, Hug your friend			▶ **Song: Shake your body!**	

3 My room (pages 24–31)

Vocabulary	Chant: Grammar	Story and value	CLIL	Thinking skills
toy box, bookcase, lamp, mat, window, door	Where's my (book)? It's in / on / under the (bookcase).	*Goodnight Dad* Being patient	Being tidy	Comparing
▶ **Total physical response:** Where's my rabbit?, Look under the mat, Look in the toy box, Ah, here it is			▶ **Song: My messy room**	

4 In the jungle (pages 32–39)

Vocabulary	Chant: Grammar	Story and value	CLIL	Thinking skills
rhino, tiger, elephant, snake, spider, crocodile	Is it a (rabbit)? Yes it is. / No, it isn't.	*The jungle* Being creative	Where animals live	Noticing details
▶ **Total physical response:** Walk through the jungle, Turn around, It's a big snake, Run away			▶ **Song: Walking through the jungle**	

5 Fruit and vegetables (pages 40–47)

Vocabulary	Chant: Grammar	Story and value	CLIL	Thinking skills
potatoes, pineapple, carrots, tomatoes, watermelon, banana	Do you like (vegetables)? Yes I do. / No I don't.	*The fruit salad* Healthy eating	Food types	Comparing, contrasting

▶ **Total physical response:** Hmm … I'm hungry, Look, there's an apple, I can't reach. Jump … Ouch	▶ **Song: Do you like vegetables?**

6 My town (pages 48–55)

Vocabulary	Chant: Grammar	Story and value	CLIL	Thinking skills
bus stop, park, school, toy shop, supermarket, zoo	Let's go to (the park).	*The present* Keeping your town clean	The environment	Creating associations

▶ **Total physical response:** It's a toyshop … wow, What's this?, Look … a robot, Oh no	▶ **Song: Come and see my town!**

7 Jobs (pages 56–63)

Vocabulary	Chant: Grammar	Story and value	CLIL	Thinking skills
farmer, police officer, builder, doctor, firefighter, teacher	My (mum)'s a (doctor).	*Fire fighters* Helping others	Jobs and vehicles	Sorting

▶ **Total physical response:** I'm a farmer, Listen … what's that?, It's a bull, Run	▶ **Song: Let's play firefighters!**

8 The weather (pages 64–71)

Vocabulary	Chant: Grammar	Story and value	CLIL	Thinking skills
rainy, windy, cold, snowy, hot, sunny	Is it (hot / cold / sunny / snowy)? Yes, it is. / No, it isn't.	*The island* Be prepared	Weather and geography	Sequencing

▶ **Total physical response:** It's a hot and sunny day … phew, Put your hat on, Eat an ice cream … yum, Oh no, the sea! Run	▶ **Song: What's the weather like today?**

9 In the countryside (pages 72–79)

Vocabulary	Chant: Grammar	Story and value	CLIL	Thinking skills
tree, leaves, frog, grass, flower, bee	The bee is / isn't (big). It's (small).	*The bee* Respecting nature	Animal habitats	Sorting

▶ **Total physical response:** I'm walking in the garden, Look, it's a flower, Look, it's a bird, Ouch! It's a tree	▶ **Song: Four frogs in a tree**

🔟 Phonics (pages 80–39)

Unit 1: 'a' cat, dad	Unit 2: 'i' sit, pin	Unit 3: 'e' bed, pen	Unit 4: 'o' dot, pot	Unit 5: 'u' cut, bus	Unit 6: 'm' mum, mat	Unit 7: 'j' jam, job	Unit 8: 'l' log, lamp	Unit 9: 'w' wet, wow	Phonics review

 pages 90–94   **Certificate:** 95   **Stickers:** End section

 www.cambridge.org/supersafari/familyfun   3

Hello!

1 CD1 02 **Listen and point. Say the names.**

4 | 1 Mike 2 Gina 3 Polly 4 Leo

3 CD1 04 05 Listen and act. Listen and colour.

Family fun!

Singing for pleasure   7

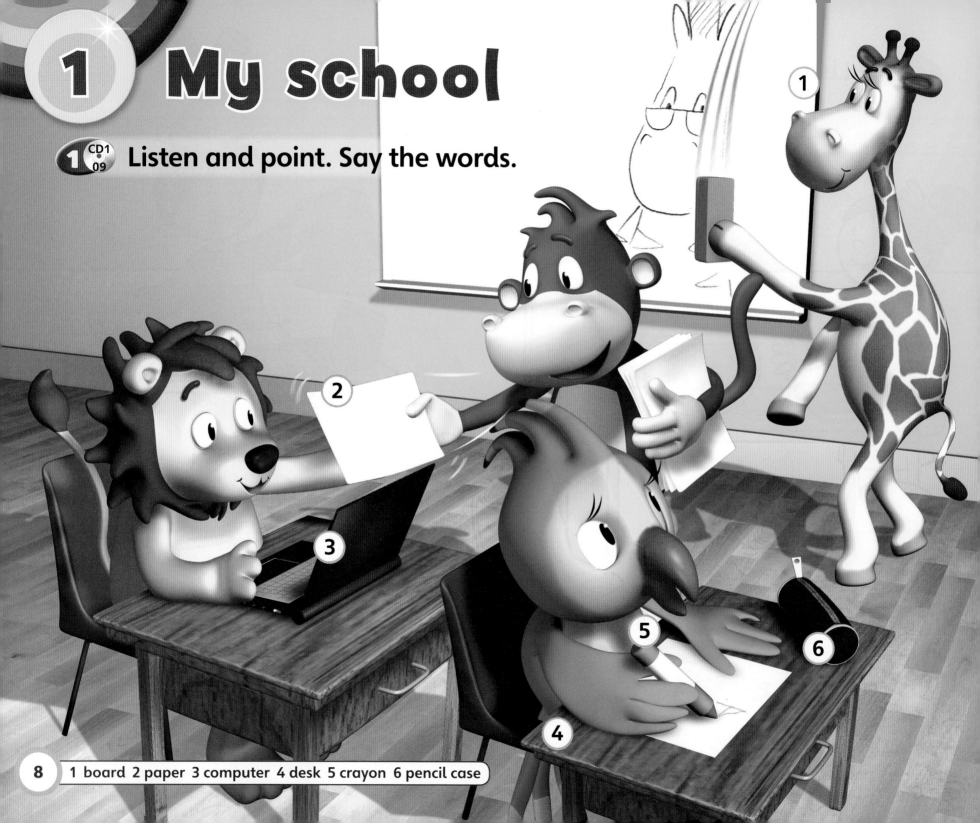

1 My school

1 CD1 09 **Listen and point. Say the words.**

1 board 2 paper 3 computer 4 desk 5 crayon 6 pencil case

2 CD1 10 **Listen and trace. Chant.**

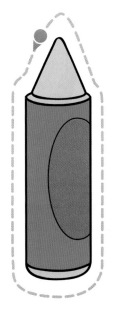

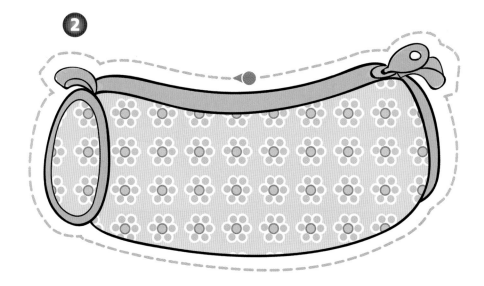

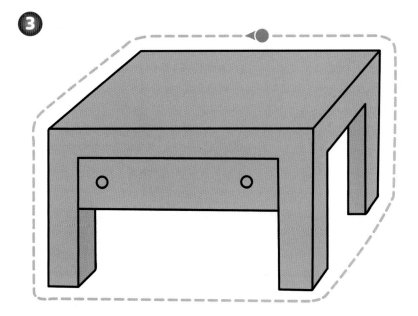

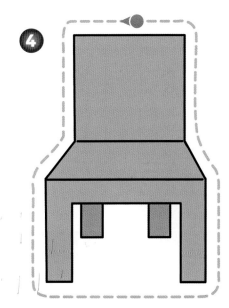

 Family fun!

This is my (crayon).   **9**

4 CD1 15 16 **Listen and sing.**

The medals

Value: Appreciating differences 13

Move your body

6 CD1 20 **Listen and point. Trace and say the words.**

1

2

3

4

7 (Think!) **Look and match. Say the actions.**

Thinking skills: Sorting   **15**

2 My body

1 arms 2 hands 3 feet 4 legs 5 body 6 head

Family fun!

I can (clap my hands).

3 Listen and act. Listen and colour.

CD1 27 28

18 Total physical response

4 CD1 30 31 **Listen and sing.**

1

2

3

4

Family fun!

Animal bodies

Listen and point. Trace and say the words.

1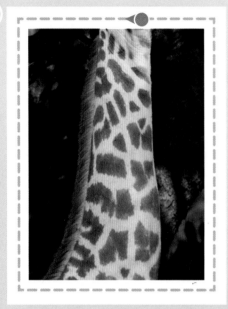

2

3

4

7 Think! **Look and match. Say the words.**

1

2

3

4

Thinking skills: Noticing details **23**

3 My room

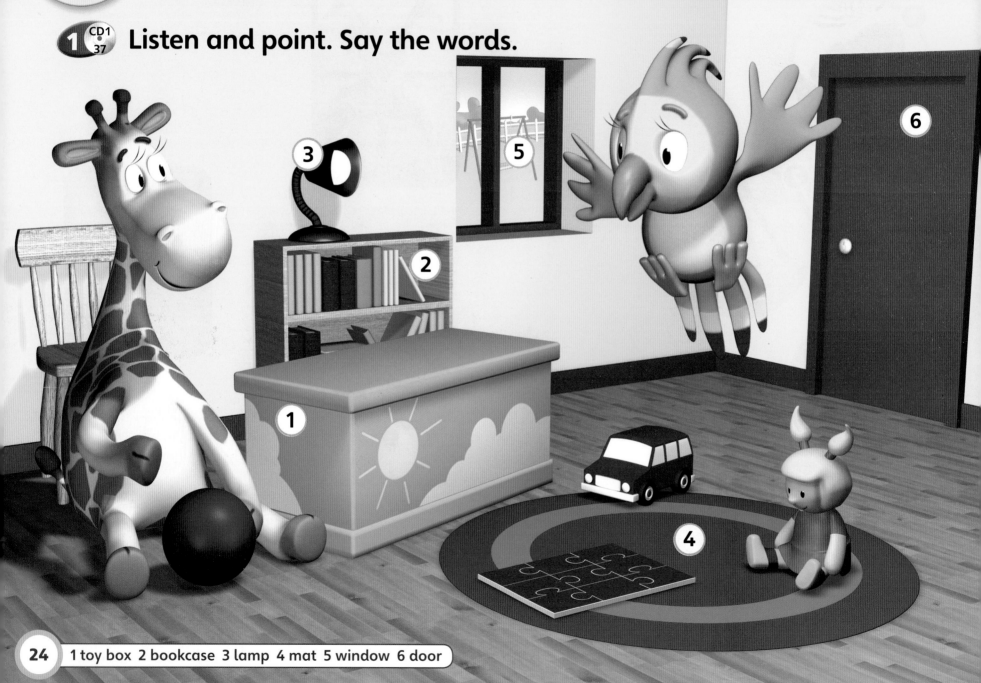

1 toy box 2 bookcase 3 lamp 4 mat 5 window 6 door

2 ^{CD1 38} Listen and circle. Chant.

1

2

Family fun!

Where's my (book)? It's in / on / under the (bookcase). **25**

Listen and act. Listen and colour.

Total physical response

4 CD1 43 44 **Listen and sing.**

Goodnight Dad

Value: Being patient

Being tidy

 6 Listen and point. Draw and say the words.

7 (Think!) **Spot the difference. Circle the objects and say.**

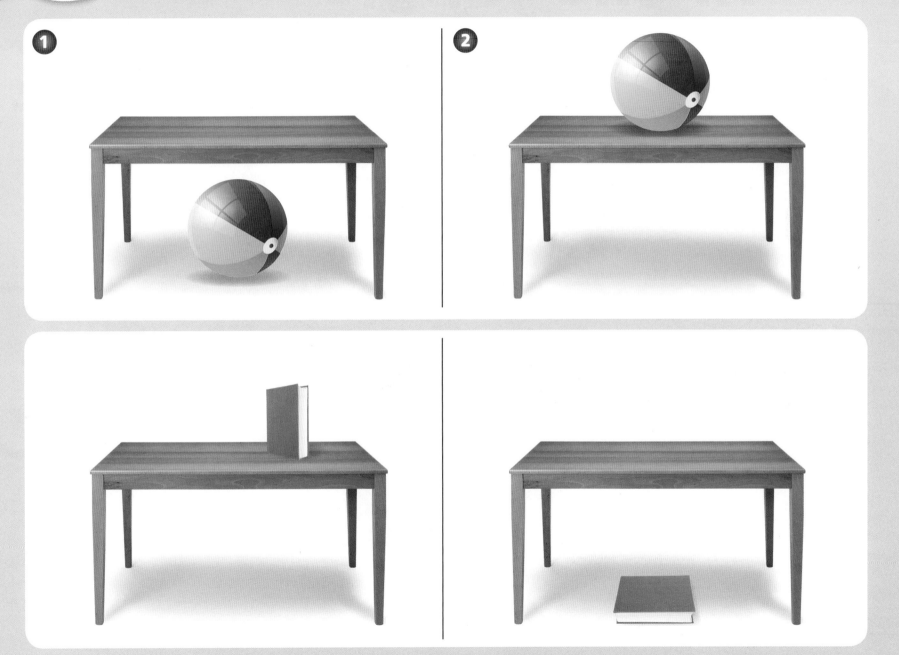

Thinking skills: Comparing **31**

4 In the jungle

1 rhino 2 tiger 3 elephant 4 snake 5 spider 6 crocodile

2 CD1 53 Listen and trace. Chant.

3 Listen and act. Listen and colour.

CD1 55 56

Total physical response

4 CD1 58 59 **Listen and sing.**

Value: Being creative 37

Where animals live

Listen and point. Trace and say the animals.

1

2

3

4

7 Think! **Look and circle. What's wrong?**

Thinking skills: Noticing details   **39**

5 Fruit and vegetables

Listen and point. Say the fruit and vegetables.

1 potatoes 2 pineapple 3 carrots 4 tomatoes 5 watermelon 6 bananas

2 CD1 67 Listen, trace and colour. Chant.

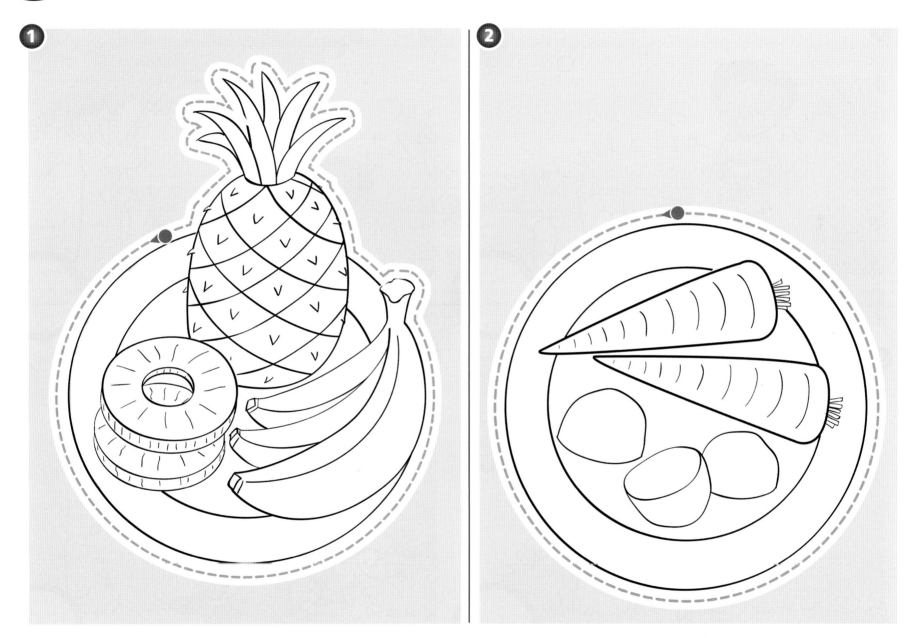

Do you like (vegetables)? Yes I do. / No, I don't.   41

3 CD2 02 03 Listen and act. Listen and colour.

Total physical response

4 CD2 05 06 Listen and sing.

The fruit salad

1

2

3

4

Food types

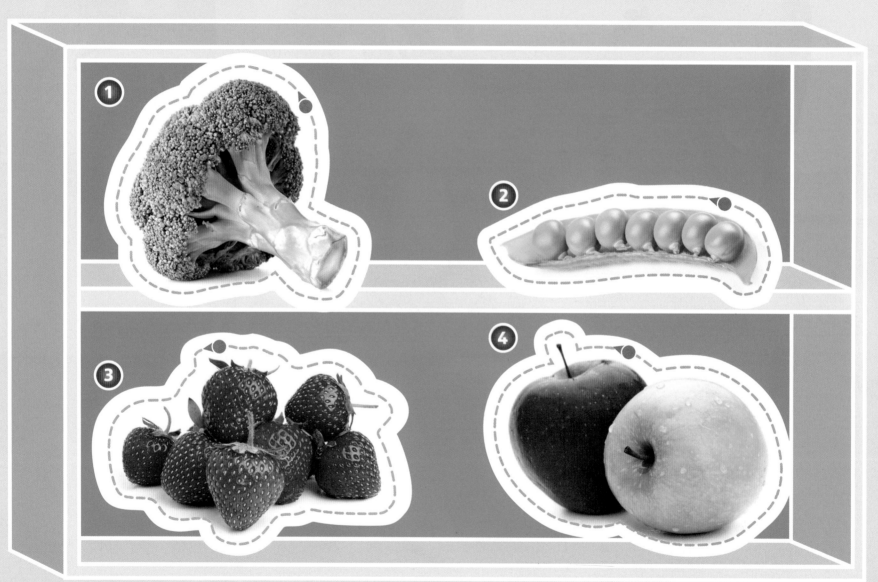

7 Think! **Look and circle the fruit.**

1

2

3

4

5

6

Thinking skills: Comparing, contrasting   **47**

6 My town

1 CD2 13 Listen and point. Say the places.

2 3 4 6 5 1

48 1 bus stop 2 park 3 school 4 toy shop 5 supermarket 6 zoo

2 CD2 14 Listen and trace. Chant.

3 Listen and act. Listen and colour.

Total physical response

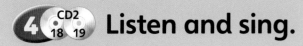

Listen and sing.

The present

1

2

3

4

Family fun!

Value: Keeping your town clean 53

The environment

 6 **CD2 23** Listen and point. Draw and say.

①

②

7 (Think!) **What's wrong? Look and circle.**

(Thinking skills: Creating associations) **55**

7 Jobs

1 CD2 25 **Listen and point. Say the jobs.**

1 farmer 2 police officer 3 builder 4 doctor 5 firefighter 6 teacher

2 CD2 26 **Listen and match. Chant.**

1

2

3 CD2 28 29 **Listen and act. Listen and colour.**

1

2

3

4

4 CD2 31 32 **Listen and sing.**

Firefighters

Jobs and vehicles

6 CD2 36 **Listen and point. Trace and say the words.**

1

2

3

4

7 (**Think!**) **Look and match. Say the words.**

1

2

3

4

Thinking skills: Sorting   **63**

1 Listen and point. Say the words.

1 rainy 2 windy 3 cold 4 snowy 5 hot 6 sunny

2 CD2 40 Listen and match. Chant.

Listen and act. Listen and colour.

Total physical response

4 Listen and sing.

The island

Weather and geography

1

2

7 **Think!** **What's next? Match and say the words.**

Thinking skills: Sequencing   **71**

⑨ In the countryside

1 CD2 51 **Listen and point. Say the words.**

1 tree 2 leaves 3 frog 4 grass 5 flower 6 bee

2 CD2 52 Listen and circle. Chant.

1

2

Family fun!

The (bee) is / isn't (big). It's (small). **73**

Listen and act. Listen and colour.

4 CD2 57 58 **Listen and sing.**

Value: Respecting nature 77

Animal habitats

Listen and point. Trace and say the words.

1

2

3

4

7 (Think!) **Look and match. Say the words.**

1

2

3

4

(Thinking skills: Sorting) **79**

1 Look and find.

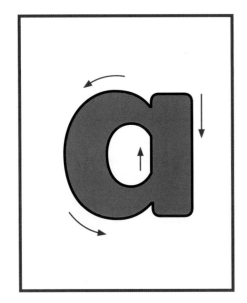

c a t

d a d

2 Listen and join in.

1 **Look and find.**

Phonics

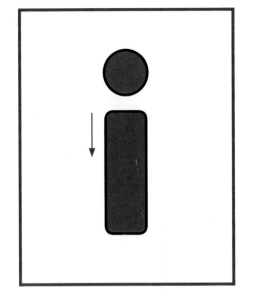

s i t

p i n

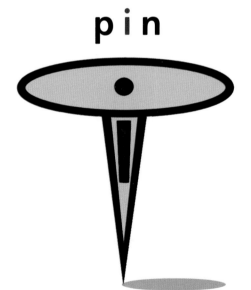

 2 **Listen and join in.**

CD1 36

1 Look and find.

b e d

p e n

2 Listen and join in.

1 **Look and find. Colour the letter.**

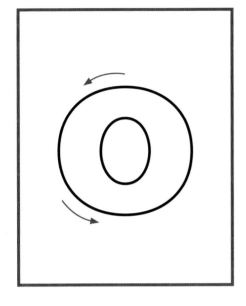

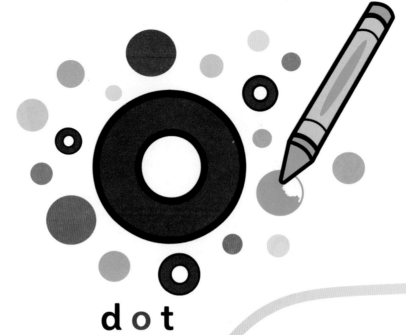

d o t

p o t

2 **Listen and join in.**

1 Look and find. Colour the letter.

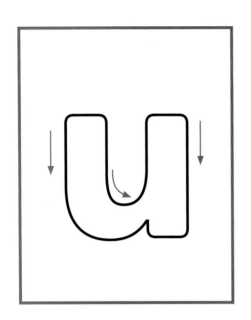

c u t

b u s

2  Listen and join in.

1 **Look and find. Colour the letter.**

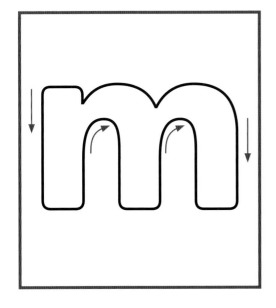

m u m

m a t

2 **Listen and join in.**

1 Look and find. Trace the letter.

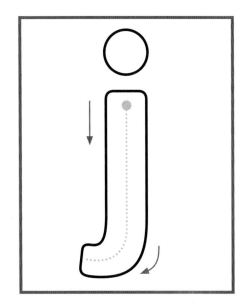

j a m

j o b

 2 Listen and join in.

1 **Look and find. Trace the letter.**

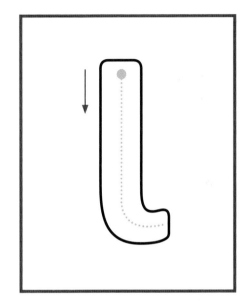

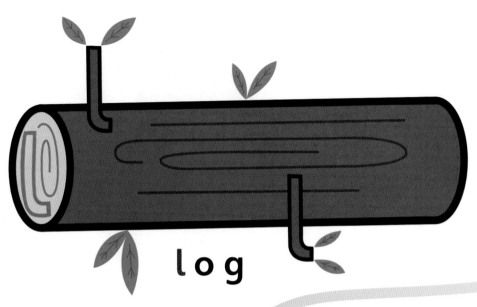

l o g

l a m p

2 **Listen and join in.**

1 Look and find. Trace the letter.

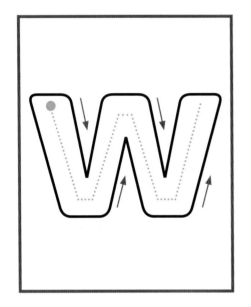

w e t

w o w

 2 Listen and join in.

Listen and play bingo.

j a m

l a m p

w e t

p o t

m a t

b u s

c a t

p i n

p e n

CD1 22 **Listen to the sentences. Colour the frames.**

1 Listen and colour the circles. Colour the frames.

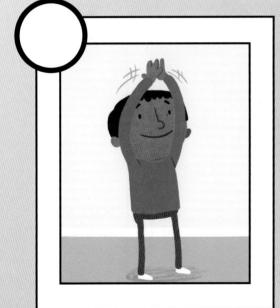

Listen and colour the circles. Colour the frames.

Listen and colour the circles. Colour the frames.

Listen and colour the circles. Colour the frames.

Well done!

....

has finished Super Safari!

Thanks and acknowledgements

Authors' thanks

The authors would like to thank a number of people who have made significant contributions towards the final form of Super Safari: Colin Sage, Helen Brock and Carolyn Wright, our editors, for their expertise in working on the manuscripts, and the support we got from them.

Our designers, Blooberry, for their imaginative layout and all the artists – in particular Bill Bolton – for the inspiring artwork that has brought our ideas to life in such beautiful ways.

Liane Grainger, Managing Editor and Emily Hird, Publisher, for their many useful suggestions for improvement.

Jason Mann, Editorial Director at Cambridge University Press, for his vision and encouragement.

The publishers are grateful to the following contributors:

Blooberry Design: cover design, book design and page make-up
Bill Bolton: cover illustration
Alison Prior: picture research
Ian Harker: audio recording and production
James Richardson: chant writing and production
Robert Lee, Dib Dib Dub Studios: song writing and production

The publishers and authors are grateful to the following illustrators:

Bill Bolton; Judy Brown; Gareth Conway (The Bright Agency); Kate Daubney; Mark Duffin; Louise Garner; Sue King (Plum Pudding Illustration); Bernice Lum

The authors and publishers acknowledge the following sources of copyright material and are grateful for the permissions granted. While every effort has been made, it has not always been possible to identify the sources of all the material used, or to trace all copyright holders. If any omissions are brought to our notice, we will be happy to include the appropriate acknowledgements on reprinting.

The publishers are grateful to the following for permission to reproduce copyright photographs and material:

p.14 (L): Alamy/© Rubberball; p.14 (TR): Superstock/© Rubberball; p.14 (BL): Alamy/© Picture Partners; p.14 (BR): Shutterstock/© Maria Mykhaliuk; p.15 (TC): Shutterstock/© Stuart Monk; p.15 (TR): Shutterstock/© Dmitri Maruta; p.15 (BC): Shutterstock/© Andresr; p.15 (BR): Shutterstock/© Natalia Matreeva; p.15 (BL): Shutterstock/© Ksenia Tupitsyna; p.15 (C): Shutterstock/© Andresr; p.15 (TL): Shutterstock/© Glenda; p.22 (TL): Shutterstock/© Sharon Haegar; p.22 (TR): Shutterstock/© apiguide; p.22 (BC): Shutterstock/© Panu Ruangian; p.22 (BR): Shutterstock/© Sh.el.Photo; p.23 (TC & 2): Shutterstock/© Pearl Media; p.23 (BR & 4): Shutterstock/© Volodymr Burdiak; p.23 (TR & 3): Shutterstock/© John Michael Evan Potter;p.23 (BC & I): Shutterstock/© Dmitrijs Mihejevs; p.30 (L): Corbis/© Jo-Ann Richards/First Light; p.30 (R): Getty Images/© Andrew Hetherington; p.31 (table): Shutterstock/© Horiyan; p.31 (ball): Shutterstock/© Mejnak; p.31 (book): Shutterstock/© StudioVin; p.38 (TL): Shutterstock/© Peter Wollinga; p.38 (TR): Shutterstock/© Andrew Burgess; p.38 (BR): Shutterstock/© Kamonrat; p.38 (BL): Shutterstock/© Praisaeng; p.46 (TL): Shutterstock/© gilmar; p.46 (TR): Shutterstock/© Mazzur/ p.46 (BL): Shutterstock/© Aleksey Troshin; p.46 (BR): Shutterstock/© Petr Malyshev; p.47 (TL): Shutterstock/© Jiri Hera; p.47 (TC): Shutterstock/© Dionisvera; p.47 (TR): Shutterstock/© Aleksey Troshin; p.47 (BL): Shutterstock/© Betacam-SP; p.47 (BC): Shutterstock/© ravl; p.47 (BR): Shutterstock/© EM Arts; p.54 (L): Shutterstock/© WDG Photo; p.54 (R): Alamy/© Gruffydd; p.62 (TL): Alamy/© Martin Bennett; p.2 (TR): Shutterstock/© Bjorn Heller; p.62 (BL): Alamy/© Martin Bennett; p.62 (BR): Shutterstock/© Daseaford; p.63 (I,2): Alamy/© eye35; p.63 (3): Corbis/© Mark Kerrison/Demotix; p.63 (4): Alamy/© Dorset Media Service; p.63 (TL): Corbis/© 237/Chris Ryan/Ocean; p.63 (TR): Alamy/© Robert Convery; p.63 (BL): Alamy/© Cultura Creative; p.63 (BR): Alamy/© Mia Caruana; p.70 (L): Shutterstock/© Volodymer Goink; p.70 (R): Shutterstock/© Microstock Man; p.78 (TL): Shutterstock/© Micha Klootwijk; p.78 (TR): Shutterstock/© Christian Kohler; p.78 (BL): Frank Lane Picture Agency/© Bill Coster; p.78 (BR): Shutterstock/© Alexey Stiop; p.79 (I) Shutterstock/© Hintau Alaksei; p.79 (2): Shutterstock/© Panbazil; p.79 (3): Shutterstock/© Irinak; p.79 (4): Shutterstock/© Jang Hongyan; p.79 (T): Shutterstock/© Ron Zmiri; p.79 (CR): Shutterstock/© M Pellinni; p.79 (CL): Shutterstock/© Konstantnin; p.79 (BR): Shutterstock/© pzAxe.